G000117686

with
DAVID HOLLIDAY
and

| GROVER DALE | SHEILA FORBES | DOROTHY REYNOLDS | MAVIS VILLIERS |
| EDITH DAY | JOHN HEWER | MARGARET CHRISTENSEN | SYDNEY ARNOLD |

Scenery & Costumes designed by **MICHAEL NORTHEN**
Lighting by **MICHAEL NORTHEN**   Musical direction by **GARETH DAVIES**
Musical numbers and Dances staged by **JOE LAYTON**
Book, Music, Lyrics & Direction by **NOEL COWARD**

From June 21st	Stalls. 30/-, 25/-, 15/-, Dress Circle 20/-, 10/-
Mons. to Fris. 8.0. Sats. 5.30 & 8.30	
Mats. Wed. 2.30	Upper Circle 10/6

The Quotable
Noel Coward

by Sheridan Morley

RUNNING PRESS
PHILADELPHIA · LONDON

A Running Press Miniature Edition™
© 1999 by Running Press
All rights reserved under the Pan-American and International
Copyright Conventions

Printed in China

British Library Cataloguing-in-Publication Data.
A catalogue record for this book is available from the British Library.

ISBN 0-7624-0642-9

This book may be ordered by mail from the publisher.
Please include £1.00 for postage and handling.
But try your bookstore first!

Running Press Ltd
c/o Biblios Publishers Distribution Services Ltd
Star Road
Partridge Glen
Horsham, West Sussex RH 13 8LD

Contents

Introduction   4

Coward on Theatre   11

Coward on Success   35

Coward on His Contemporaries   59

Coward at Large   83

Coward on Life   107

Introduction

Although it has been an
utter delight to put together
these quotations from the
playboy of the West End world
and the master of all its enter-
tainment trades, to celebrate
the Coward centenary, I am
a little daunted at the thought
of giving them so brief an
introduction. It took me about

a hundred thousand words
to write his (and my) first
biography, *A Talent to Amuse*,
back in 1969, and in the years
since there has scarely passed a
day on which I haven't wanted   5
to add a few more.

Born within a few days
of the last Christmas of the
previous century, hence the
name Noel, Coward was a
boy actor by the age of ten.

By the time he was fifteen, he had acted in D. W. Griffith's silent film, *Hearts of the World.* At twenty, he was a produced playwright, and by the time he was thirty he had written *The Vortex, Cavalcade, Private Lives,* and *Bitter Sweet,* among countless other plays, revues, musicals and operettas. By the time Coward was forty he had written, directed, and

6

starred in the Academy-Award winning film *In Which We Serve*. At fifty he was painting, writing short stories and novels, singing in cabaret, and starring in plays and films, many of which he also wrote and directed.

By the time he was sixty he was legendary, and when he died at 73 in 1973, it was already clear that he had

represented not just the entire
history of British popular
theatre in his lifetime, but
the spirit of the century.

8   He was also one of the
kindest and funniest men I
ever knew. When he asked
me to write his life story, he
agreed that he would not even
look at it until it was in print.
I sent him the first copy and
waited in some trepidation

for his reply. It came as a cable I still have framed above my desk. "I am", it read, "simply wild about me". Me too.

Sheridan Morley

NEW THEATRE

For ONE WEEK COMMENCING MONDAY, FEBRUARY

Nightly at 6.0 Mats.: Wednesday & Saturday at 2.0 'Phone: 4

Prices of Admission—Reserved: Stalls 7/–, 6/–, 5/–, Circle

5/–, 4/–, 3/–, Balcony 2/6. Unreserved: 1/6, 1/–, (Including

H. M. TENNENT LTD. in association with JOHN C. WILSON

ANNOUNCE

PERSONAL APPEARANCE

OF

NOEL COWARD

IN HIS OWN PLAYS

"PRESENT LAUGHTER"

(Prior to London Production)

"THIS HAPPY BREED"

(Prior to London Production)

"BLITHE SPIRIT"

(Now in its 2nd year at the Duchess Theatre, London)

JOYCE CAREY

Chapter One

COWARD

ON THEATRE

On a Drury Lane musical of
Gone With the Wind:

12

**They should cut two things,
the second act and
the child's throat.**

On Lionel Bart's *Blitz* musical:

Just as long as the real thing
and twice as noisy.

On the opening night of
Lerner and Loewe's *Camelot*:

14

**Very like *Parsifal*, but
without the jokes.**

On a plan for an all-star gala
to be called *Summer Stars*:

Some, I fear, are not.

Advice to a young actor:

16

Just say the lines and try not to trip over the furniture.

17

About a chorus boy who had
failed to remember to wear
18   something under his tights:

**For God's sake get that boy
to take that Rockingham tea
service out of his trousers.**

On being told by an actress
rehearsing one of his plays
that she knew his lines
'backwards last night':

**And that's just the way
you are saying them
this morning.**

To an actress who resolutely picked
her nose during an audition:

**Good-bye my dear, and do remember
to wave when you get to the bridge.**

20

Coward on Theatre

To an actress who threatened
in rehearsal to throw
something at him:

**You might start, my dear,
with my cues.**

On the first night on Broadway of his play *This Was a Man* in 1926:

Everybody who was anybody was there . . . at least until the first interval.

22

On a cabaret tour of South
Africa during World War II:

**We agreed that my accompa-
nist Norman Hackforth
would play a five-minute
intermission medley of
my tunes; this would allow
me briefly to retire to
my dressing room and
consider whether or
not to shoot myself.**

23

On being told, 'Mr. Coward,
I'm the star of your new film
Bunny Lake Is Missing.   79
I'm Keir Dullea':

**Keir Dullea,
gone tomorrow.**

I try never to write plays
for the intelligentsia or
for critics—sixteen
performances and you
close on Saturday week.

28

To a Hollywood producer:

**Terribly sorry, unable write
life of Florence Nightingale** 29
**for Gertrude Lawrence,
as am busy writing life of
Joan of Arc for Mae West.**

31

30   For 500 dollars, I would gleefully
turn *War and Peace* into
a music-hall sketch.

On playwriting:

Consider the public; treat it with tact and courtesy and it will accept much from you, if you are clever enough to win it to your side. Never fear it or despise it. Coax it, charm it, interest it, stimulate it, shock it now and then if you must; make it laugh and cry and think, but above all never, never bore the living hell out of it.

32

The most important
ingredients for any play
are life, death, food, sex
and money, though not
necessarily in that order.

The theatre must be treated
with respect; it is a place
of strange enchantment, a
temple of dreams; what it
most emphatically is not
is a scruffy, ill-lit hall
serving as a temporary
platform for political
or social propaganda.

COWARD
ON SUCCESS

**Television is for appearing
on, not for watching.**

On seeing himself for the first
time on television:

**Someone appears to have
sat on my head.**

Everyone but Somerset
Maugham said I was the
second Somerset Maugham;   37
he said he preferred to
think of me as the
second Sacha Guitry.

Success took me to
her bosom like a
maternal boa constrictor.

Asked if there was anything
he could not do:

40   **Well, I still can't saw ladies
in half, or perform on
the trapeze; but I'm
working on it.**

Coward on Success

To a fan, who told him she had just
finished re-reading his memoirs:

**Quite right, Madam; one should
always stay abreast of the classics.**

Coward on Success

I became extraordinarily unspoiled by
my great success with
The Vortex in 1924: as a
matter of fact I still am.

In 1924 *The Vortex* made my name
as an actor and playwright, which was
just as well, as until then I had
not proved myself to be so
hot in either capacity.

44

I was photographed, interviewed and photographed again. In the street. In the park. In my dressing room. With my dear old mother. Without my dear old mother. And, on one occasion, sitting in an over-elaborate bed looking . . . heavily doped. . . .

This last photograph did me, I
believe, considerable harm; everyone
assumed I was in the last stages of
drug addiction and that they had bet-
ter hurry to see me in my play before
my inevitable demise placed that
dubious pleasure beyond their reach.

48   I can take any amount of criticism, as
      long as it is unqualified praise.

The most difficult thing of
all is to have a big hit very
early in your playwriting
career. Suddenly you're the
belle of the ball, and then
they go for you and, equally
suddenly, chop chop.

49

50   I was a talented child, God knows, and when washed and smarmed down a bit, passably attractive; but I was, I believe, one of the worst boy actors ever inflicted on the paying public.

Looking back on his career:

**I cannot offhand think
of anyone who was more
intimately or turbulently
connected with our
theatre in the 1920s.**

52

My faith in my own talents remained unwavering, but it did seem unduly optimistic to assume that American theatregoers of the 1920s would be 53 perceptive enough to see me in the same brilliant light that I saw myself. In this I was, as usual, absolutely right. They didn't.

54

Private Lives was variously described in the press as 'thin, brittle, iridescent and delightfully daring' all of which connotated to the public mind cocktails, evening dress and irreverent allusions to copulation, thereby causing a gratifying number of perfectly respectable people to queue up at the box office.

56 Throughout the 1930s I was a highly publicised and irritatingly successful figure, much in demand.

On his last major
Broadway musical:

I don't know what the
**world is coming to, but
it is definitely NOT
coming to *Sail Away*.**

COWARD
ON HIS CONTEMPORARIES

On the Edwardian producer
J. R. Crawford:

60

**He directed rehearsals with all
the airy deftness of a rheumatic
deacon producing *Macbeth*
for a church social.**

On Randolph Churchill:

Dear Randolph, so unspoiled by his great lack of success.

On Prime Minister
Neville Chamberlain:

A good Lord Mayor for Birmingham in a bad year.

62

On being told that the petite
Ivy St. Helier, star of his
Bitter Sweet, was unable to
play, as she had broken her
leg in two places:

I had no idea it had two places.

Coward on His Contemporaries

To Evelyn Laye, just before
the Broadway first night
of his *Bitter Sweet*,
giving her an elegantly
wrapped cage:

I wanted to be the first to
give you the bird. Now
remember, you have nothing
at all to worry about.
Everything and everyone just
depends on you, that's all.

64 Gertrude Lawrence lived her entire life in an imaginary screening room, forever watching her own rushes.

Anna Neagle playing Queen Victoria always made me think that Albert must have married beneath him.

On working with Claudette Colbert:

66

**I'd wring her neck,
if only I could find it.**

To a woman in a restaurant who told him he must remember her, they had first met with Douglas Fairbanks:

Madam, there are days when I don't even remember Douglas Fairbanks.

Ian Fleming's cooking always tasted to me like armpits.

(The two authors once shared a house   69
in Jamaica which, because of the rising
damp, Noel christened 'Goldeneye,
nose and throat'.)

On being told by Cary Grant
'I'm Cary Grant':   71

**But of course you are,
dear boy.**

To Clifton Webb, who was proving
inconsolable over the death
of his aged mother:

72

You really must pull yourself
together Clifton, and stop all this
weeping; it is not, after all, entirely
unusual to be orphaned at 72.

On seeing a cinema
poster advertising
Michael Redgrave and
Dirk Bogarde in *The Sea* 73
Shall Not Have Them:

**I fail to see why not;
everyone else has.**

After telling Elaine Stritch to
arrive suitably dressed and
sober at an important
backer's cocktail party:

**I told you to behave, not
to come dressed like a
fucking geography teacher.**

To John Gielgud in rehearsals
for *Nude with Violin*:

75

**The more you cry on stage,
dear boy, the less they'll cry
in the audience.**

On Peter O'Toole's performance as
Lawrence of Arabia:

**If he'd been any prettier, they'd have
had to call it Florence of Arabia.**

To his godson, Daniel Massey,
who played Noel in the film *Star*
with Julie Andrews:

Too many 'dear boys' dear boy.

Young playwrights would 26 do well to compare their reviews with their royalty statements.

To a forgetful Dame Edith Evans
during National Theatre rehearsals
for his *Hay Fever* in 1965:

The line, dear Dame, is 'On a clear   81
day you can see Marlowe'. On a VERY
clear day, as you persist in saying,
you can see Marlowe *and*
Beaumont *and* Fletcher.

QUEEN'S THE

SHAFTESBURY AVENUE, W.1.

Licensed by the Lord Chamberlain to PRINCE
General Manager: FREDERICK CAR

EVENINGS at 8.0   MATINEES: THURSDAYS and

H. M. Tennent Ltd. presents

NOËL COWARD'
SUITE IN THREE K

LILLI
PALMER

NOËL
COWARD

in

A SONG AT TWILIGHT

A play in two acts

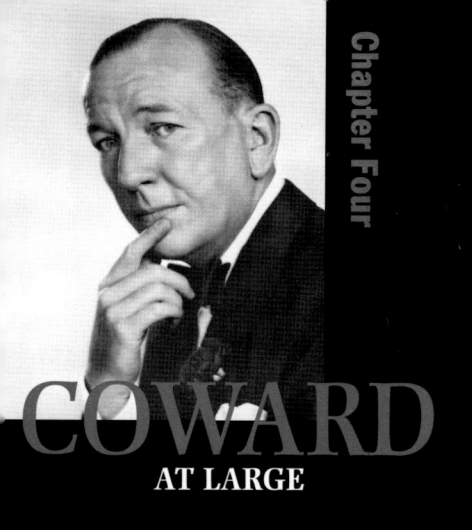

Chapter Four

COWARD

AT LARGE

Trying to send a cable to Gertrude
Lawrence for one of her Broadway
first nights, Noel decided to sign it
in the name of the then Mayor of
New York, Fiorello LaGuardia:

**Telephone operator: But are you
really Mayor LaGuardia?**

Noel: No.

Operator: In that case you certainly

may not sign the cable LaGuardia.
What is your real name?

Noel: Noel Coward.

Operator: Are you really   85
Noel Coward?

Noel: Yes.

Operator: In that case you may sign
the cable LaGuardia.

86 **I have always had a
Ritz mind.**

88 Asked by Gillette, in a celebrated
series of magazine advertisements,
to list whatever in his view
had true style:

Coward at Large

A candy-striped jeep, Jane Austen,
Cassius Clay, Monsieur de Givenchy,
The Times before it changed, a Zebra
(but not a Zebra Crossing),
evading boredom, Gertrude Lawrence,
the Paris Opera House, White,
a seagull, a Brixham trawler,
Margot Fonteyn, any Cole Porter
song, English pageantry,
Marlene's voice and
Lingfield racecourse has a tiny bit.

To a reporter, asking him if he
had anything witty to say to
the *Melbourne Star*:

Kangaroo.

91

∞

To a reporter in London,
asking if he had anything
to say to the *Evening Star*:

Twinkle.

92   **If a person over fifty tries to
be 'with it', they usually
end up without it.**

I care a very great deal about
the human race; it is, when   93
all is said and done,
all we have got.

On his arrival in Turkey:

**I am of course known here
as English Delight.**

On the habit of American
newspapers of referring to
'a trained nurse' and
'a friendly drink':

**What would be the purpose
of an untrained nurse or
an unfriendly drink?**

I have never cared for either
squid or octopus; like
eating hot india rubber.

98

At the beginning of World War II,
I was sent to Paris to explain to the
French the policy of His Majesty's
Government. As it didn't then seem to
have one, there was not a lot to do.

On the wartime plan to drop
Home Office leaflets into
enemy territory:

**If it is now the policy of
Mr. Churchill's government
to bore the Germans to
death, I am not entirely
sure we have the time.**

100   The Eye of Heaven has only ever
meant anything to me when it winks.

102

Do I believe in God?
Well, let's just say we
have reached a tentative
working agreement.

Wit is like caviar, it should be
served in very small portions,
not sloshed about.

Coward at Large

In London, at the Café de Paris,
I sang to café society; in Las Vegas,
at the Desert Inn, I sang to
Nescafé society.

Let's hope we have no
worse to plague us
Than two shows a night
in Las Vegas.

BY NOEL COWARD

Cavalcade

CHARLES B. COCHRAN
PRESENTS

IN ASSOCIATION WITH
THEATRE ROYAL
DRURY LANE

ATS. MON. WED. & SAT. AT 2

Photography and Illustration Credits

Archive Photos: pp. 59, 70.

Archive Photos/Popperfoto: pp. 55, 94.

Columbia (Courtesy Kobal): p. 77.

Culver Pictures: front cover and pp. 17, 28, 38.

Gainsborough (Courtesy Kobal): p. 101.

By courtesy of the Mander and Mitchenson
Theatre Collection: back cover and
pp. 1, 10, 34, 42, 51, 58, 67, 80, 82, 83,
87, 90, 104, 106, 107, 113, 120, 122.

Detail of Noel Coward
by Dorothy Wilding, by courtesy of the
National Portrait Gallery, London: p. 11.

By courtesy of the
National Portrait Gallery, London: pp. 114, 127.

Paramount (Courtesy Kobal): pp. 24–25, 46–47.

Two Cities (Courtesy Kobal): p. 35.

I don't look back in anger, nor in
anything approaching even mild rage;
I rather look back in pleasure and   125
amazement and amusement at
the way my life has gone. It really
has all been most enjoyable.

Asked how he would like
124   to be remembered:

**By my charm, of course,
you silly bugger.**

Coward on Life

All one hopes in old age is that one's friends make it through lunch.

My body has certainly wandered a good deal these last 50 years, but I have the uneasy suspicion that my mind has not wandered nearly far enough.

For those readers of my work who
wish I would just stop writing, I fear
the future is very bleak indeed.

Asked how the public
would know when he had   119
retired from the theatre:

They can follow my coffin.

118   The only way to enjoy one's life is to work; work is so much more fun than fun.

I behaved throughout World War II
with gallantry, tinged I suspect with
the strong urge to show off.

117

116

**Most of my gift horses
seem to have come
with very bad teeth.**

**The definition of
a perfect life?
Mine.**

But I believe, that since my life
began, the most I've had is just a
talent to amuse. (*Bitter Sweet*, 1929)

Coward on Life

I have a very slight urge to
reform, but I have cunningly
always suppressed it.

112

I never cared who scored the goal
Or which side won the silver cup;
I never learned to bat or bowl
But I heard the curtain going up.

I was born in Teddington, an ordinary middle-class little boy. I was not gutter, I never gnawed kippers' heads in the street, as Gertrude Lawrence quite untruthfully claimed that *she* did. But nor was my first memory the crunch of carriage wheels on the drive. Because we hadn't got a drive.

The world has treated me
very well; but then I haven't
treated it so badly either.

I am always being told on my travels
of something I have just missed;
I get to Japan just after the Cherry
Blossom has fallen; I reach Canada
just when the foliage has gone;
people are always telling me of
something I have just failed to see.
I find this very restful.

COWARD

ON LIFE